THE OFFICIAL BIRMINGHAM CITY Annual 2010

Written by Pete Oliver

A Grange Publication

Printed in the EU.

ISBN 978-1-906211-73-8

£6.99

Birmingham City

FOUNDED:	1875
HOME:	St. Andrew's
CAPACITY:	30,009
CLUB NICKNAME:	The Blues
MANAGER:	Alex McLeish
HONOURS:	Football League Championship: Promoted 2007, 2009 Division One: Promoted 2001/02 (play-offs) Division Two: Champions 1892/93, 1920/21, 1947/48, 1954/55 Runners-up 1893/94, 1900/01, 1902/03, 1971/72, 1984/85 Division Three: Champions 1994/95, Runners-up 1991/92 FA Cup: Runners-up 1931, 1956 League Cup: Winners 1963, Runners-up 2001 Leyland Daf Cup: Winners 1991 Auto Windscreens Shield: Winners 1995 European Inter-Cities Fairs Cup: Runners-up 1959/60, 1960/61
FORMER NAMES:	1875 Small Heath Alliance, 1888 Small Heath, 1905 Birmingham, 1945 Birmingham City
GROUNDS:	1875 Arthur Street, 1877 Muntz Street, Small Heath, 1906 St. Andrew's
RECORD ATTENDANCE:	66,844 v Everton, FA Cup 5th round, February 1939
RECORD LEAGUE GOALSCORER:	Joe Bradford (1920-35) 249
MOST LEAGUE APPEARANCES:	Frank Womack (1908-28) 491
RECORD TRANSFER FEE RECEIVED:	£6.5 million from Liverpool for Jermaine Pennant, August 2006.
RECORD TRANSFER FEE PAID:	Undisclosed to Santos Laguna for Christian Benitez, June 2009.

Contents

Introduction

Welcome to the 2010 Birmingham City Annual!

Well, what a memorable year that was and a proud one for everyone connected with Birmingham City.

Gaining promotion last season wasn't always plain-sailing of course, but then nothing worth achieving is ever handed to you on a plate.

We had to show great character, determination, togetherness and skill to successfully negotiate the marathon that is the Championship. Now we can look forward to the next challenge, which is to try and re-establish ourselves in the Premier League.

The 2009/10 season will be my first full campaign in the English top-flight and it is one I am really looking forward to. It will be a great test for all of us to go head-to-head with some of the best club sides in the world and to try and compete.

We will need total commitment from everyone and your unfailing support if we are to achieve our goals.

My aim is to build a team that can handle the special demands of the Premier League and try and gain a foothold in the league which will allow the club to continue to go from strength to strength.

Hopefully the players we have assembled will provide some more fantastic moments along the way and we can enjoy the ride together. Enjoy the annual and here's to another successful season.

Alex McLeish

Promotion Party

Blues took their promotion crusade right to the wire before clinching a place back in the Premier League in the most dramatic style possible with victory on the final day of the season.

After battling it out with local rivals Wolves for the Championship title in the early part of the season, Alex McLeish's men then had to set their sights on securing the second automatic promotion place.

Reading, Sheffield United and Cardiff City also had their eyes on the prize and by the final day of a gripping 2008/09 campaign it had boiled down to a straight fight between Reading, the Blues and the Blades.

Birmingham looked as though they might have blown their chance by losing at home to Preston in their penultimate game.

But knowing they needed a victory in a winner-takes-all clash at Reading to guarantee

promotion, Alex McLeish's men responded superbly to secure a famous 2-1 win at the Madejski Stadium.

With Sheffield United being held to a 0-0 draw at Crystal Palace a single point would have been enough to take Blues back up to the top flight at the first time of asking.

But on a tension-wracked afternoon the players and fans didn't know that until the final whistle, so goals from Keith Fahey and Kevin Phillips went down in Blues' history and sparked a promotion party both in Berkshire and Birmingham.

"The fans have been behind us all season, they have been brilliant," enthused striker Cameron Jerome. "It means a lot to everyone involved with the club."

Promotion Party

waitrose.com
PUMA
PHILLIPS
PREMIER LEAGUE
F&C

McLeish Magic

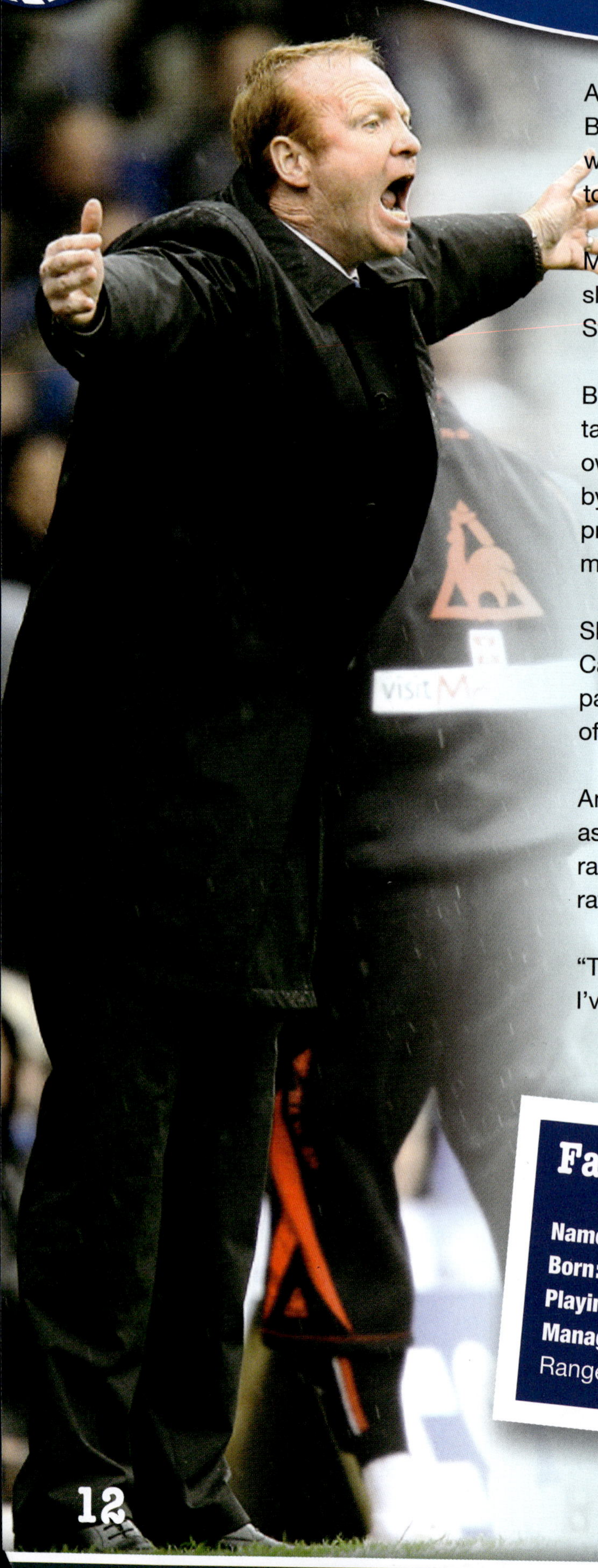

Alex McLeish added his name to the list of Birmingham's most celebrated managers when he guided the Blues to promotion back to the Premier League at the first attempt.

McLeish was unable to stop the Blues sliding to relegation when he took charge at St. Andrew's in November 2007.

But the canny Scot proved he has what it takes when he had the chance to mould his own team and produce a winning formula by swiftly banishing those memories with promotion from the Championship 18 months later.

Shrewd signings like Kevin Phillips, Lee Carsley, Keith Fahey and Stephen Carr all paid off, while McLeish also got the best out of longer established Blues favourites.

And McLeish, known in football circles as 'Big Eck', made no secret of where he ranked the top-two finish in a league he rates as one of the toughest in the world.

"This was up there with every achievement I've had in the game," he said.

Factfile

Name: Alex McLeish
Born: Barrhead, Scotland 21/01/59
Playing career: Aberdeen, Motherwell
Managerial career: Motherwell, Hibernian, Rangers, Scotland, Birmingham City

For a man who won league titles in his native Scotland both as a player and a manager, and who won 77 caps for his country before becoming national team manager, that is some statement.

And the good news for Blues fans is that McLeish wants to carry on his good work at St. Andrew's – dismissing rumours that he might leave at the end of the 2008/09 season.

"I'm looking forward to building a team equipped to cope with the Premier League," he said.

"We know the challenge is huge but we're not looking at it as difficult or daunting. We're talking about embracing the challenge."

Becoming a force again in the Premier League might be a tough task – but at least Blues know they are in good hands.

Blues Managerial History

	From	To
Alex McLeish	**Nov 2007**	**Present**
Steve Bruce	2001	2007
Trevor Francis	1996	2001
Barry Fry	1993	1996
Terry Cooper	1991	1993
Lou Macari	1991	1991
Dave Mackay	1989	1991
Garry Pendrey	1987	1989
John Bond	1986	1987
Ron Saunders	1982	1986
Jim Smith	1978	1982
Sir Alf Ramsey	1977	1978
Willie Bell	1975	1977
Fred Goodwin	1970	1975
Stan Cullis	1965	1970
Joe Mallett	1965	1965
Gil Merrick	1960	1964
Pat Beasley	1959	1960
Arthur Turner	1954	1958
Bob Brocklebank	1949	1954
Harry Storer	1945	1948
George Liddell	1933	1939
Leslie Knighton	1928	1933
William Harvey	1927	1928
Billy Beer	1923	1927
Frank Richards	1915	1923
Bob McRoberts	1910	1915
Alec Watson	1908	1910
Alfred Jones	1892	1908

How Promotion Was Won

The Blues enjoyed another memorable season in 2008/09 as they again proved that you can't keep a good team down. Follow their route to instant promotion back to the Premier League as the drama unfolded month by month for Alex McLeish and his men.

August

Birmingham City 1, Sheffield United 0
Wycombe Wanderers 0, Birmingham City 4 (Carling Cup)
Southampton 1, Birmingham City 2
Birmingham City 2, Barnsley 0
Southampton 2, Birmingham City 0 (League Cup)
Norwich City 1, Birmingham City 1

Blues made the perfect start to their bid to bounce back into the top flight on the opening day of the season – although they left it late to do it.

New signing Kevin Phillips gave a taste of things to come as he came off the bench to grab an injury-time winner against Sheffield United, while Maik Taylor enjoyed a first clean sheet since Boxing Day 2007.

Alex McLeish then rang the changes for a comfortable Carling Cup win at Wycombe, which featured first Blues goals for Mehdi Nafti and debutant Quincy Owusu-Abeyie.

Back on Championship duty, Blues came from behind to secure a first win at Southampton for 25 years when ex-Saint Phillips sunk his former club with another super-sub performance after Garry O'Connor had cancelled out Chris Perry's strike.

The perfect start continued when Barnsley were despatched 2-0 at St. Andrew's with Phillips, getting his first start, and O'Connor again the men on target.

Defeat at Southampton in the Carling Cup swiftly curtailed that adventure and although Blues dropped their first league points in a 1-1 draw at Norwich following a Seb Larsson goal, they ended August joint top of the table with Wolves and Preston.

September

Birmingham City 1, Doncaster Rovers 0
Bristol City 1, Birmingham City 2
Birmingham City 0, Blackpool 1
Cardiff City 1, Birmingham City 2
Derby County 1, Birmingham City 1

Following a break for international action, Cameron Jerome opened his account with the winner for ten-man Blues against Doncaster after Nafti had been sent off.

And there looked to be no stopping McLeish's men when an own-goal and another for Jerome, coupled with some fine saves from Taylor, earned victory at Ashton Gate.

But the first hiccup of the promotion campaign came against Blackpool, when Blues surrendered their unbeaten start with a shock home defeat.

Bouncing back, Blues went to promotion rivals Cardiff to secure an important victory thanks to James McFadden's first goal of the season and an impressive strike from Owusu-Abeyie.

And another stunning effort from the on-loan Owusu-Abeyie secured a point from a 1-1 draw at Derby to keep Blues in second spot by the end of the month.

October

Birmingham City 1, Queens Park Rangers 0
Burnley 1, Birmingham City 1
Birmingham City 1, Crystal Palace 0
Birmingham City 3, Sheffield Wednesday 1
Queens Park Rangers 1, Birmingham City 0

Blues got back to winning ways at home against QPR courtesy of a typically predatory strike from Phillips which briefly took them into top spot before Blues picked up a valuable point at Turf Moor when Jerome came off the bench to cancel out Burnley's lead.

And another solitary goal was enough to beat Crystal Palace back at St. Andrew's as a last-gasp winner deflected in by O'Connor extended Blues' impressive home record and took them to the top of the table.

Franck Queudrue made his first start of the season and stayed in the side as Wednesday were then blown away in a breath-taking first-half performance which brought two more goals for O'Connor and another for Phillips.

But Blues' unbeaten away record then finally came to an end when ten-man QPR gained swift revenge for their defeat at the start of the month by reversing the scoreline and allowing Wolves to resume pole position at the head of the Championship.

November

Birmingham City 0, Coventry City 1
Nottingham Forest 1, Birmingham City 1
Birmingham City 3, Charlton Athletic 2
Swansea City 2, Birmingham City 3
Birmingham City 2, Ipswich Town 1
Wolverhampton Wanderers 1, Birmingham City 1

A busy November didn't get off to the best of starts when former Birmingham striker Clinton Morrison headed in to give Coventry victory as Nicky Hunt made his Blues' debut after signing on loan from Bolton.

McLeish also gave a first start to loan man Nigel Quashie next up at Forest and Blues gained a creditable point thanks to McFadden's early goal.

And a first win in four games followed in spectacular style against Charlton when McFadden curled in a wonder goal, Phillips scored on his 500th career appearance and Queudrue capped a fine fight-back with his first goal for the club before Quashie's dismissal saw Blues finish the game with ten men.

The trip to Swansea was almost as eventful as McLeish's men mounted a superb comeback to hand the Welshmen a rare home defeat. Marcus Bent scored his first Blues goal before 'Super Kev' Phillips turned the game round after coming off the bench, nodding in and then grabbing the points with a 20-yard cracker.

Blues then made it a hat-trick of wins against Ipswich thanks to a fine volley from Liam Ridgewell and a ninth goal of the season for the prolific Phillips.

And even though Wolves were opening up a gap at the top of the table, the leaders were held by Blues at Molineux where Jerome scored first in a 1-1 draw in front of over 26,000 fans.

December

Birmingham City 3, Watford 2
Plymouth Argyle 0, Birmingham City 1
Preston 1, Birmingham City 0
Birmingham City 1, Reading 3
Ipswich 0, Birmingham City 1
Birmingham City 0, Swansea City 0

A typically hectic December revealed the first serious hiccups in the Blues promotion push, although the month started well enough as Phillips, Bent, with his first home goal, and Jerome were all on target to sting the Hornets.

Captain Lee Carsley's stunning first Blues goal then earned another away win at Plymouth but Preston proved too tough a nut to crack at Deepdale as Jon Parkin grabbed an injury-time winner.

And promotion rivals Reading then won the big game at St. Andrew's to oust Blues from second place as another Phillips goal was not enough to prevent a biggest home defeat of the season.

Blues fans did at least have a happy Christmas thanks to a Boxing Day success at Ipswich, sealed by the season's first penalty converted by McFadden, which saw club captain Damien Johnson back in action for the first time following a back injury.

But that was to prove a rare win in a sticky mid-winter spell as the year ended with a goalless draw against Swansea after David Murphy was sent off.

January

Birmingham City 0, Wolves 2 (FA Cup)
Birmingham City 1, Cardiff City 1
Blackpool 2, Birmingham City 0
Birmingham City 1, Derby County 0
Sheffield Wednesday 1, Birmingham City 1

After a frozen pitch had delayed the third-round FA Cup derby clash with Wolves, injury-hit Blues swiftly bowed out but new loan signing Lee Bowyer struck late to secure an important point against top-six rivals Cardiff as the Championship programme resumed.

Bogey-side Blackpool and former Blue DJ Campbell then made it an unhappy trip to the seaside but again Birmingham bounced back with a crucial victory over Derby when ex-Ram Carsley headed in the decisive goal as McLeish shook up his side in search of a winning formula.

Consistency proved elusive as Blues then had to settle for a point at Hillsborough but it felt like a good one as Phillips struck three minutes into added time to head the equaliser and cap a much improved performance.

February

Birmingham City 1, Burnley 1
Birmingham City 2, Nottingham Forest 0
Coventry City 1, Birmingham City 0
Crystal Palace 0, Birmingham City 0

Solid if unspectacular through February, Blues reclaimed the second automatic promotion place which they would only briefly relinquish again.

In-form Burnley stole a march at St. Andrew's but they were pegged back by that man Phillips again and Blues were back to winning ways against Forest thanks to Bent and a first goal for the club for Irishman Keith Fahey which made it a sweet St Valentine's Day.

Coventry then completed the double over their Midlands neighbours as Blues lost for the first time in five, and it was stalemate at Selhurst Park to end the month as ten-man Palace held on to stop Birmingham, who included new signing Stephen Carr, from closing the gap on stuttering Wolves.

March

Sheffield United 2, Birmingham City 1
Birmingham City 1, Bristol City 0
Birmingham City 1, Southampton 0
Barnsley 1, Birmingham City 1
Doncaster 0, Birmingham City 2
Birmingham City 1, Norwich City 1

A controversial late penalty led to defeat at Bramall Lane as the Blades moved their promotion challenge into top gear after a Chris Morgan own-goal looked as though it would give Blues a valuable point.

But back on home turf Blues produced one of their best performances of the season to beat Bristol City and go back above Reading into second spot. McLeish's men dominated but needed a late header from Queudrue to seal the points.

Southampton were then beaten by the same scoreline thanks to a Fahey finish and Blues again proved their resilience by striking late at Barnsley through a rare Martin Taylor strike to sustain an unbeaten run that would extend to nine games at a critical stage of the season.

A rapid return to South Yorkshire brought maximum points at Doncaster thanks to a Jerome header, a first Blues goal for on-loan forward Hameur Bouazza and another clean sheet for the evergreen Maik Taylor.

And even though struggling Norwich cancelled out Jerome's goal to bring an end to Blues' three-match winning home run by the end of the month, promotion was still on the cards.

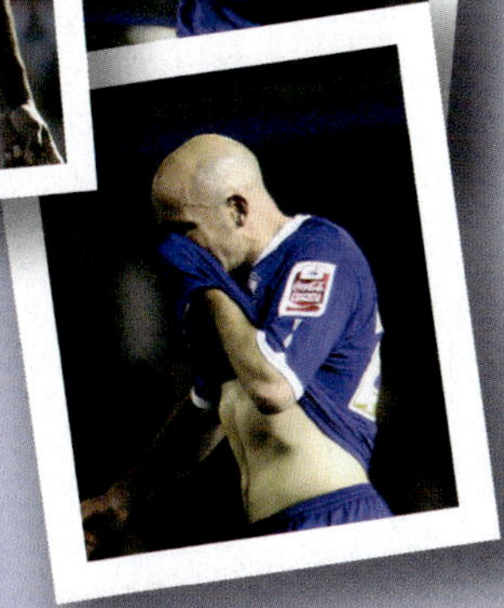

April

Birmingham City 2, Wolves 0
Charlton Athletic 0, Birmingham City 0
Birmingham City 1, Plymouth Argyle 1
Watford 0, Birmingham City 1
Birmingham City 1, Preston 2

The biggest crowd of the season at St. Andrew's was treated to a famous win as the Blues started their final push for promotion in style. Captain Carsley was sent off in the first half but despite being a man short, champions-elect Wolves were sent packing by goals from Jerome and the fit-again O'Connor.

Relegation-bound Charlton put up stern resistance next up at The Valley but a stunning late save by Maik Taylor secured another vital point.

Taylor was again the centre of attention against Plymouth but this time the keeper was controversially sent off as Blues had to battle back from going behind to a penalty and losing Liam Ridgewell to a broken leg. Substitute Queudrue headed the equaliser to calm some of the nerves starting to mount as the race for the second promotion place threatened to become a four-horse race.

Blues kept their noses in front with a priceless win at Watford when Jerome bagged his tenth goal of the season thanks to a deflected shot which set up a potential promotion decider against strong-finishing Preston.

Blues knew victory in front of a full house would take them back to the promised land of the Premier League and everything was going according to plan when Fahey headed them in front.

But after Bowyer and Preston's Lee Williamson were sent off, two wonder goals from Preston killed the party and took the drama into the final day of the season.

May

Reading 1, Birmingham City 2

Birmingham, Reading and Sheffield United were all chasing automatic promotion but Blues had their destiny in their own hands and they responded heroically to grab their place back in the top flight and subject their rivals to the play-off lottery.

With United drawing at Palace, it was winner-takes-all at the Madejski Stadium and it was the Blues who grabbed the moment to cap a memorable season.

Fahey and Phillips scored the decisive goals either side of half-time and even though Reading pulled one back, McLeish's braves held out to spark scenes of celebration in Berkshire and back home in Birmingham.

MAIK TAYLOR

Stat Attack

Blues Results 2008/09

Sat 09 Aug	**Sheffield United**	**H**	League	W 1-0	Phillips 90	24,019
Wed 13 Aug	Wycombe Wanderers	A	Carling Cup	W 4-0	Nafti 14; Larsson 64; Jerome 73; Owusu-Abeyie 86	2,735
Sat 16 Aug	Southampton	A	League	W 2-1	O'Connor 49; Phillips 77	18,925
Sat 23 Aug	**Barnsley**	**H**	League	W 2-0	Phillips 13; O'Connor 45	17,413
Tue 26 Aug	Southampton	A	Carling Cup	L 0-2		11,331
Sat 30 Aug	Norwich City	A	League	D 1-1	Larsson 40	24,229
Sat 13 Sep	**Doncaster Rovers**	**H**	League	W 1-0	Jerome 46	18,165
Tue 16 Sep	Bristol City	A	League	W 2-1	Carey 8og; Jerome 24	18,456
Sat 20 Sep	**Blackpool**	**H**	League	L 0-1		20,983
Sat 27 Sep	Cardiff City	A	League	W 2-1	McFadden 5; Owusu-Abeyie 41	18,304
Tue 30 Sep	Derby County	A	League	D 1-1	Owusu-Abeyie 26	29,743
Sat 04 Oct	**Queens Park Rangers**	**H**	League	W 1-0	Phillips 45	18,498
Sat 18 Oct	Burnley	A	League	D 1-1	Jerome 77	13,809
Tue 21 Oct	**Crystal Palace**	**H**	League	W 1-0	O'Connor 90	17,706
Sat 25 Oct	**Sheffield Wednesday**	**H**	League	W 3-1	O'Connor 11,15; Phillips 38	17,300
Tue 28 Oct	Queens Park Rangers	A	League	L 0-1		13,594
Mon 03 Nov	**Coventry City**	**H**	League	L 0-1		17,215
Sat 08 Nov	Nottingham Forest	A	League	D 1-1	McFadden 13	21,415
Sat 15 Nov	**Charlton Athletic**	**H**	League	W 3-2	McFadden 13; Phillips 50; Queudrue 55	20,071
Fri 21 Nov	Swansea City	A	League	W 3-2	Bent 42; Phillips 74,79	16,956
Tue 25 Nov	**Ipswich Town**	**H**	League	W 2-1	Ridgewell 9; Phillips 14	15,689
Sat 29 Nov	Wolverhampton Wanderers	A	League	D 1-1	Jerome 48	26,329
Sat 06 Dec	**Watford**	**H**	League	W 3-2	Phillips 8; Bent 18; Jerome 85	18,174
Tue 09 Dec	Plymouth Argyle	A	League	W 1-0	Carsley 62	10,446
Sat 13 Dec	Preston North End	A	League	L 0-1		10,943
Sat 20 Dec	**Reading**	**H**	League	L 1-3	Phillips 60	19,695
Fri 26 Dec	Ipswich Town	A	League	W 1-0	McFadden 39p	23,536
Sun 28 Dec	**Swansea City**	**H**	League	D 0-0		21,836
Tue 13 Jan	**Wolverhampton Wanderers**	**H**	F.A. Cup	L 0-2		22,232
Sat 17 Jan	**Cardiff City**	**H**	League	D 1-1	Bowyer 90	19,853
Sat 24 Jan	Blackpool	A	League	L 0-2		8,105
Tue 27 Jan	**Derby County**	**H**	League	W 1-0	Carsley 59	15,330
Sat 31 Jan	Sheffield Wednesday	A	League	D 1-1	Phillips 90	18,409
Sat 07 Feb	**Burnley**	**H**	League	D 1-1	Phillips 37	16,763
Sat 14 Feb	**Nottingham Forest**	**H**	League	W 2-0	Bent 62; Fahey 75	17,631
Sat 21 Feb	Coventry City	A	League	L 0-1		22,637
Tue 24 Feb	Crystal Palace	A	League	D 0-0		12,847
Sun 01 Mar	Sheffield United	A	League	L 1-2	Morgan 74og	24,232
Wed 04 Mar	**Bristol City**	**H**	League	W 1-0	Queudrue 87	17,551
Sat 07 Mar	**Southampton**	**H**	League	W 1-0	Fahey 45	16,735
Tue 10 Mar	Barnsley	A	League	D 1-1	M.Taylor 85	11,299
Sat 14 Mar	Doncaster Rovers	A	League	W 2-0	Jerome 19; Bouazza 42	11,482
Sat 21 Mar	**Norwich City**	**H**	League	D 1-1	Jerome 38	18,159
Mon 06 Apr	**Wolverhampton Wanderers**	**H**	League	W 2-0	Jerome 45; O'Connor 69	25,935
Sat 11 Apr	Charlton Athletic	A	League	D 0-0		20,022
Mon 13 Apr	**Plymouth Argyle**	**H**	League	D 1-1	Queudrue 50	19,323
Sat 18 Apr	Watford	A	League	W 1-0	Jerome 73	16,180
Sat 25 Apr	**Preston North End**	**H**	League	L 1-2	Fahey 57	24,825
Sun 03 May	Reading	A	League	W 2-1	Fahey 19; Phillips 60	23,879

Stat Attack

Championship Table 2008/09

Team	P	Home W	Home D	Home L	Home F	Home A	Away W	Away D	Away L	Away F	Away A	Pts	Goal Diff
Wolverhampton	46	15	5	3	44	21	12	4	7	36	31	90	28
Birmingham	46	14	5	4	30	17	9	9	5	24	20	83	17
Sheff Utd	46	12	6	5	35	22	10	8	5	29	17	80	25
Reading	46	12	5	6	40	17	9	9	5	32	23	77	32
Burnley	46	14	5	4	42	23	7	8	8	30	37	76	12
Preston	46	16	3	4	39	20	5	8	10	27	34	74	12
Cardiff	46	14	5	4	40	23	5	12	6	25	30	74	12
Swansea	46	11	9	3	40	22	5	11	7	23	28	68	13
Ipswich	46	8	9	6	30	26	9	6	8	32	27	66	9
Bristol City	46	7	13	3	30	23	8	3	12	24	31	61	0
QPR	46	12	7	4	28	19	3	9	11	14	25	61	-2
Sheff Wed	46	11	6	6	26	14	5	7	11	25	44	61	-7
Watford	46	11	6	6	42	32	5	4	14	26	40	58	-4
Doncaster	46	9	5	9	16	18	8	2	13	26	35	58	-11
Crystal Palace	46	9	8	6	26	19	6	4	13	26	36	57	-3
Blackpool	46	5	8	10	25	33	8	9	6	22	25	56	-11
Coventry	46	8	8	7	26	26	5	7	11	21	32	54	-11
Derby	46	9	7	7	31	26	5	5	13	24	41	54	-12
Nottm Forest	46	8	7	8	27	28	5	7	11	23	37	53	-15
Barnsley	46	8	7	8	28	24	5	6	12	17	34	52	-13
Plymouth	46	7	5	11	31	35	6	7	10	13	22	51	-13
Norwich	46	9	5	9	35	28	3	5	15	22	42	46	-13
Southampton	46	4	10	9	23	29	6	5	12	23	40	45	-23
Charlton	46	6	8	9	33	38	2	7	14	19	36	39	-22

Blues Appearances 2008/09

Player	League		FA Cup		League cup		Other	
G Agustien	13 (5)	0	1 (0)	0	1 (0)	0	0 (0)	0
S Aydilek	0 (0)	0	0 (0)	0	0 (0)	0	0 (0)	0
M Bent	16 (17)	3	1 (0)	0	1 (0)	0	0 (0)	0
H Bouazza	9 (7)	1	0 (0)	0	0 (0)	0	0 (0)	0
L Bowyer	17 (0)	1	0 (0)	0	0 (0)	0	0 (0)	0
S Carr	13 (0)	0	0 (0)	0	0 (0)	0	0 (0)	0
L Carsley	41 (0)	2	1 (0)	0	2 (0)	0	0 (0)	0
C Costly	3 (5)	0	0 (0)	0	0 (0)	0	0 (0)	0
U De la Cruz	0 (1)	0	0 (0)	0	0 (0)	0	0 (0)	0
C Doyle	1 (1)	0	0 (0)	0	2 (0)	0	0 (0)	0
K Fahey	15 (4)	4	0 (0)	0	0 (0)	0	0 (0)	0
N Hunt	9 (2)	0	0 (0)	0	0 (0)	0	0 (0)	0
R Jaidi	30 (0)	0	1 (0)	0	0 (0)	0	0 (0)	0
C Jerome	25 (18)	9	1 (0)	0	0 (1)	1	0 (0)	0
D Johnson	8 (1)	0	0 (1)	0	0 (0)	0	0 (0)	0
S Kelly	2 (3)	0	0 (1)	0	1 (0)	0	0 (0)	0
A Krysiak	0 (0)	0	0 (0)	0	0 (0)	0	0 (0)	0
S Larsson	35 (3)	1	0 (0)	0	1 (0)	0	0 (0)	0
D Lyness	0 (0)	0	0 (0)	0	0 (0)	0	0 (0)	0
Maik Taylor	45 (0)	0	1 (0)	0	0 (0)	0	0 (0)	0
M Martin Taylor	23 (1)	1	0 (0)	0	1 (0)	0	0 (0)	0
J McFadden	22 (8)	4	0 (0)	0	0 (0)	0	0 (0)	0
M McPike	0 (0)	0	0 (0)	0	0 (0)	0	0 (0)	0
G McSheffrey	3 (3)	0	0 (0)	0	2 (0)	0	0 (0)	0
D Murphy	28 (2)	0	0 (0)	0	2 (0)	0	0 (0)	0
J Mutch	0 (0)	0	0 (0)	0	0 (1)	0	0 (0)	0
M Nafti	6 (5)	0	0 (0)	0	1 (0)	1	0 (0)	0
G O'Connor	10 (6)	6	0 (0)	0	2 (0)	1	0 (0)	0
Q Owusu-Abeyie	12 (7)	2	0 (0)	0	1 (1)	1	0 (0)	0
S Parnaby	19 (2)	0	1 (0)	0	2 (0)	0	0 (0)	0
K Phillips	24 (12)	14	0 (0)	0	1 (1)	0	0 (0)	0
N Quashie	8 (2)	0	1 (0)	0	0 (0)	0	0 (0)	0
F Queudrue	23 (2)	3	1 (0)	0	0 (1)	0	0 (0)	0
L Ridgewell	36 (0)	1	1 (0)	0	2 (0)	0	0 (0)	0
A Sammons	0 (0)	0	0 (0)	0	0 (0)	0	0 (0)	0
R Shroot	0 (0)	0	1 (0)	0	0 (0)	0	0 (0)	0
S Sinclair	8 (6)	0	0 (0)	0	0 (0)	0	0 (0)	0
D Traore	2 (1)	0	0 (0)	0	0 (0)	0	0 (0)	0
J Wilson	0 (1)	0	0 (0)	0	0 (0)	0	0 (0)	0
	Apps	Goals	Apps	Goals	Apps	Goals	Apps	Goals

Prize Guys

Awards Special

Blues' promotion-winning stars were honoured for their magnificent efforts during the 2008/09 season at a glittering awards night at the Birmingham ICC.

Defender Franck Queudrue capped a fantastic season by winning the Player of the Year award.

Captain Lee Carsley was rewarded for leading from the front by being voted by his team-mates as the Players' Player of the Year.

The popular Carsley also got the vote from the club's young fans as he was named Junior Blues Player of the Season.

Kevin Phillips was another double winner as the super striker picked up the Top Scorer award and the Goal of the Season prize for his stunning effort against Reading at St. Andrew's.

Garry O'Connor's goal in the home derby win over Wolves earned him a special prize for Moment of the Season.

Promising young defender Jacob Rowe got his share of the limelight as he was named Academy Player of the Year.

Supporter of season: Helen Wills

Junior Blues player: Lee Carsley

Birmingham Mail readers' player of the season: Franck Quedrue

Top scorer: Kevin Philips

Moment of the season: Garry O'Connor

Goal of the season: Kevin Philips

Academy player of the year: Jacob Rowe

Player of the season: Franck Quedrue

Players' player: Lee Carsley

Stephen Carr

Carr in the Fast Lane with Blues

Blues defender Stephen Carr thought he would have been watching the Premier League on Match of the Day.

But following a dramatic comeback, the former Republic of Ireland international is now helping Alex McLeish's side try and gain a foothold back in the top-flight of English football.

Carr is no stranger to the territory after racking up more than 300 Premier League matches for Tottenham and Newcastle United.

And that experience will be invaluable to the Blues following his surprise arrival at St. Andrew's in February.

Carr came out of retirement to help McLeish's men to promotion and his performances at right-back were so impressive that he was rewarded with a new two-year contract in the summer.

And the Dublin-born defender is delighted to be back in business.

"I thought I would be okay, but I really missed playing," Carr admitted.

"You think you can walk away from it but after 17 years and when you are only 33 you realise that there is a lot still there to be done.

"This was an unbelievable opportunity which I thought would never come around."

Carr's impact in the Blues' right-back role following injuries to Stuart Parnaby and Stephen Kelly's loan move to Stoke made him one of McLeish's best signings of the season.

And the Blues boss was delighted that his hunch paid off.

"His hunger has been superb ever since he arrived," said McLeish. "He is a fully motivated player with the kind of quality that counts in the Premier League.

"He is always positive and says the right things. He has got a winner's attitude."

Factfile

Name: Stephen Carr
Born: Dublin, 29/08/76
Position: Defender
Championship appearances 2008/09: 13
Goals: 0

Investments

Keith Fahey

Fahey Fairytale takes Keith to the Top

Keith Fahey's remarkable rise up the footballing ladder hit new heights when his goal at Reading on the final day of the 2008/09 season helped take the Blues back into the Premier League.

Less than 12 months after playing for Irish club St Patrick's Athletic, Fahey is now eyeing up Manchester United, Chelsea, Liverpool and Aston Villa as his opposition.

For the young midfielder, making it to the top tier of English football is a reward for his perseverance and for Blues boss Alex McLeish vindication of his decision to take a gamble on the 2008 Irish Player of the Year.

Fahey started his career in England with Arsenal before a brief spell at Villa Park failed to lead to a professional career.

However, great success in Ireland earned him a second bite at the cherry and after extensive research McLeish took the plunge and signed Fahey on a three-and-a-half year deal in January 2009.

"I feel that Keith will have the bit between his teeth to show he can cut it in English football," said the Blues' boss.

McLeish was proved right as Fahey played an increasingly important part in Birmingham's promotion success, scoring four goals at crucial times to suggest that he can also make his mark in the Premier League after landing his dream move.

"When it became apparent Birmingham were in for me I jumped at the chance as it's a club that's really going places," Fahey explained.

"It was a great opportunity and challenge for me to keep working hard and improving as a player."

Factfile

Name: Keith Fahey
Born: Dublin, 15/01/83
Position: Midfielder
Championship appearances 2008/09: 15 (4 subs)
Goals: 4

Barry Ferguson

James McFadden

Six of the Best

Blues blazed their way to promotion with some fabulous goals and here we've picked six of the best from 2008/09. Hope you agree!

1

Flying winger Quincy Owusu-Abeyie only stayed for six months at St. Andrew's but still made a big impression and bagged a couple of spectacular strikes.

The Ghanaian, who was on loan from Spartak Moscow, got one of those in a 2-1 win at Cardiff when he collected a throw-in from David Murphy before lashing a first-time shot from the corner of the penalty area past Bluebirds keeper Tom Heaton.

2

James McFadden normally posts at least one contender for goal of the season and this year was no exception thanks to his effort in Blues' dramatic 3-2 home win over Charlton.

McFadden opened the scoring when he cutely lifted the ball away from an Addicks' defender before curling a beauty past goalkeeper Nicky Weaver.

3

Defenders aren't normally known for their spectacular goals but Liam Ridgewell produced one out of the top drawer as Blues' promotion bid gathered pace with a win against Ipswich.

Collecting a loose ball on the corner of the penalty area, Ridgewell let fly with a volley which rocketed into the top corner of Richard Wright's net.

4

Captain Lee Carsley scored just twice in the promotion campaign but both proved to be match-winners.

And his first for the Blues at Plymouth was a cracker as he fizzed a long-range effort past Romain Larrieu to bag the points.

Top-scorer Kevin Phillips provided both quality and quantity in the Blues' promotion charge and received the official Goal of the Season award for this effort against Reading.

It came in a home defeat just before Christmas but the striker's run and 25-yard thunderbolt would have graced any game.

5

6

Kevin Phillips might have scored better goals in his season's tally of 14 but none was more important than the promotion clincher at Reading on the final day.

Needing victory to guarantee a place in the Premier League, Phillips produced a typically clinical finish to give Blues a 2-0 lead and the breathing space to secure the three points that sent them up.

Spot the Ball

ANSWERS ON PAGE 61

Bowyer's Back

Blues had a familiar face back on duty for their Premier League programme when Lee Bowyer made his move to St. Andrew's permanent.

The tough-tackling midfielder played a key part in Birmingham's promotion success in 2009 during a lengthy loan spell from West Ham.

So when the Hammers agreed to let the Londoner leave on a free transfer, Blues boss Alex McLeish wasted no time in snapping Bowyer up on a two-year deal.

Birmingham became the fifth club of Bowyer's career as the former England international brought his valuable experience and will-to-win to the Blues midfield.

"He's a proven player and you don't often get a player of Lee's calibre for nothing these days," said McLeish.

"We believe he's certainly still got the ability to justify his status as a Premier League player."

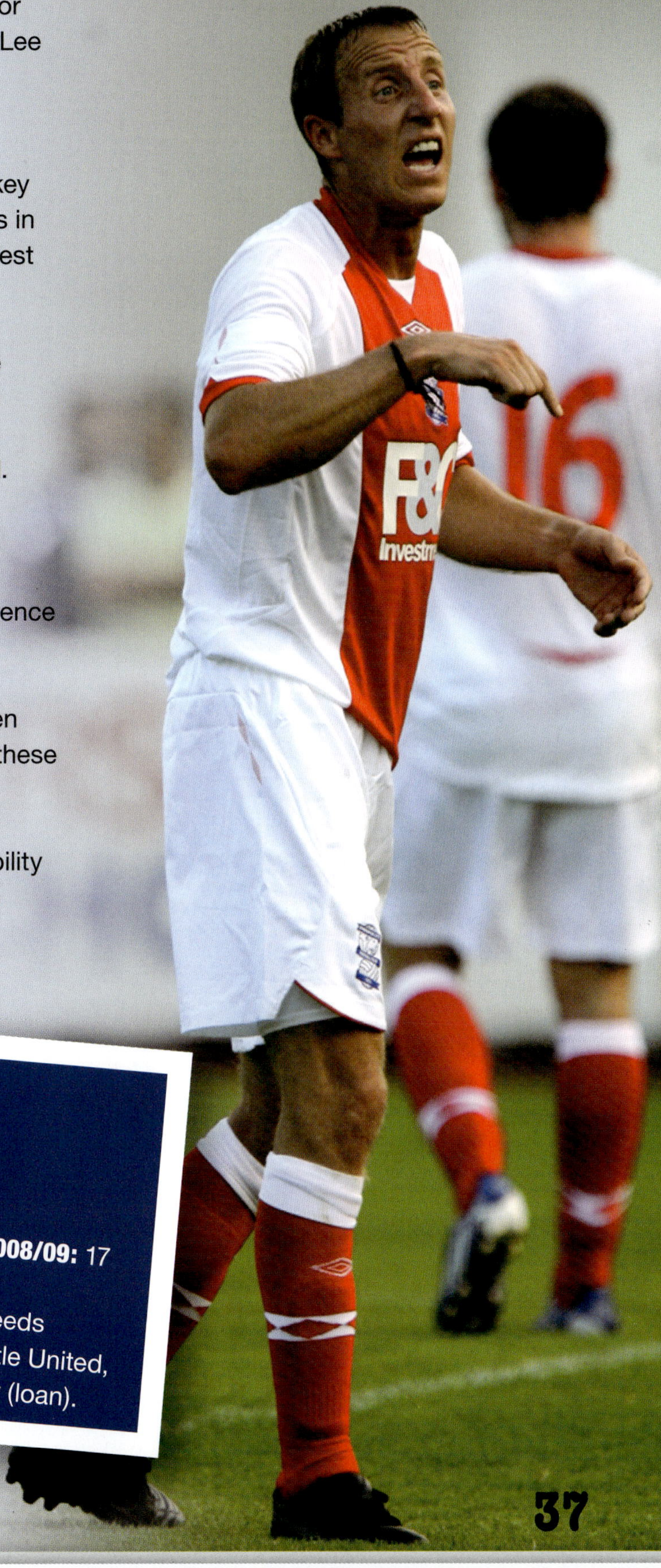

Factfile

Name: Lee Bowyer
Born: London, 03/01/77
Position: Midfielder
Blues' Championship appearances 2008/09: 17
Goals: 1
Previous clubs: Charlton Athletic, Leeds United, West Ham United, Newcastle United, West Ham United, Birmingham City (loan).

LEE
BOWYER

Big Blues Quiz

Test your knowledge of the Blues with this fun quiz.

1. How many points did Blues get to seal promotion to the Premier League in 2009?

2. After Kevin Phillips, who was Blues' second leading scorer in the 2008/09 season?

3. Which was defender Stephen Carr's last club before he came out of retirement to join Birmingham?

4. After which former Blues great did the club name the Railway Stand?

5. What country does former Blues loan player Carlos Costly play for?

6. From which club did Lee Bowyer and Nigel Quashie join on loan in the 2008/09 season?

7. What nationality is Blues Player of the Year Franck Queudrue?

8. Blues midfielder Damien Johnson passed a major international milestone for Northern Ireland in March 2009. What was it?

9. With which English club did Blues midfielder Keith Fahey start his career?

10. Against which club did captain Lee Carsley score his first goal for the Blues during the 2008/09 season?

ANSWERS ON PAGE 61

Lee Carsley

Leading from the Front

Blues fan Lee Carsley had to bide his time before playing for his hometown club but proved it was worth the wait by leading the team to promotion in his first season at St. Andrew's.

Carsley was a Premier League regular for six years at Everton following earlier top-flight spells with Coventry, Blackburn and Derby County.

His aim was to play his way back up there when he joined the Blues before the start of the 2008/09 season and he duly delivered with some outstanding performances which earned him the Player of the Year award from his team-mates.

"That's what I wanted, to play in the Premier League with Birmingham," said the Blues' captain.

Carsley admitted that it wasn't always an easy ride but praised the players and manager Alex McLeish for sticking together and staying focused on their goal.

A sending-off against Wolves kept Carsley out for three big games during the final run-in but the tough-tackling midfielder was back for the deciding game at Reading when his experience helped Blues over the line.

And now the former Republic of Ireland international is determined to play his part in keeping Birmingham in the big league and avoid the one-season stay they endured last time round.

"We want to be a stable club and show the fans that," added Carsley, who is just the kind of man Blues need to achieve that goal.

Factfile

Name: Lee Carsley
Born: Birmingham, 28/02/74
Position: Midfielder
Championship appearances 2008/09: 41
Goals: 2

F&C
Investments

South American Sizzlers

Blues will again be rocking to the samba beat of South America thanks to the sensational signing of Christian Benitez and fellow countryman Giovanny Espinoza.

The two Ecuador internationals checked into St. Andrew's during the summer to continue a colourful history of imports from their home continent.

Blues stunned the football world back in 1978 when they signed Argentina international Alberto Tarantini.

The fiery defender didn't last long at St. Andrew's but Birmingham had broken new ground in overseas transfers to start a trend which has since seen English football flooded with foreign stars.

Blues also went South American when signing Brazil striker Marcelo a decade ago and more recently Steve Bruce gambled on the talents of Uruguayan international Walter Pandiani.

Current Blues boss Alex McLeish has also been prepared to spread his net far and wide and in Benitez he believes he has discovered a striking gem.

Factfile

Name: Christian Benitez
Born: Quito (Ecuador), 01/05/86
Position: Striker
Previous clubs: El Nacional (Ecuador), Santos Laguna (Mexico)

Blues splashed out a club record fee to bring the exciting frontman from Mexican club Santos Laguna, surpassing the £6.25 million paid for Emile Heskey in 2004.

Benitez, whose father Ermen was also a prolific goalscorer for his country, was seen as a rising star of world football after banging in the goals in Mexico and McLeish headed off the chasing pack to secure his services on a three-year deal.

With experience of the 2006 World Cup finals behind him, the pacy Benitez is rated as one of Ecuador's finest ever prospects and given the chance to spearhead Blues' assault on the Premier League he now has the chance to light up English football as well.

At the other end of the field, Espinoza could make just as much of an impact as part of McLeish's new-look defence.

The powerful central defender arrived at St. Andrew's from Ecuadorian side Barcelona Sporting Club with bags of experience.

The second-most capped player in his country's history, Espinoza has played in two World Cup finals tournaments and as well as club football in Ecuador, Brazil and Mexico had a spell in the Netherlands with Vitesse Arnhem a couple of years ago.

That and the presence of Benitez should help him settle at St. Andrew's and Espinoza was delighted to add Blues to his footballing CV.

He said: "It's a new step in my career and I hope I can help the team. I'm very much looking forward to playing for this club.

"My objective is first of all to help the club remain in the Premier League and I hope to play as much as possible."

Alex McLeish on Christian Benitez: "Christian has great potential. He's small but powerful. He's a young, hungry and confident player."

Factfile

Name: Giovanny Espinoza
Born: Charguacayo (Ecuador), 12/04/77
Position: Defender
Previous clubs: Aucas, LDU Quito (Ecuador), Monterry (Mexico), Vitesse Arnhem, Cruzeiro (Brazil), Barcelona Sporting Club (Ecuador).

Come in Number One

Alex McLeish's desire for fierce competition in his squad was perfectly illustrated in his summer swoop for goalkeeper Joe Hart.

Veteran keeper Maik Taylor has been a magnificent servant for Blues and the long-serving Northern Ireland international won't give up his first-team jersey without a fight.

But by signing Hart on a season-long loan from Manchester City, McLeish showed that no-one could rest on their laurels following promotion to the Premier League.

Hart has already proved he is one of the outstanding young goalkeepers in the country, clocking up 50 top-flight starts for City since signing from Shrewsbury Town in May, 2006.

The England under-21 international, capped once at senior level by Fabio Capello, is hungry for more so leaped at the chance to move to St. Andrew's after losing his starting place at City to Shay Given.

Wolves were also in the hunt for the young shot-stopper but Blues was his preferred option with the prospect of first-team football under the guidance of McLeish and goalkeeping coach Andy Watson sure to benefit both Birmingham and Hart's burgeoning career.

Factfile

Name: Joe Hart
Born: Shrewsbury, 19/04/87
Position: Goalkeeper
Previous clubs: Shrewsbury, Tranmere (loan), Blackpool (loan), Manchester City.

Scotland the Brave

When Blues boss Alex McLeish was looking for leaders to take Birmingham back into the Premier League, it was no surprise when he returned to former club Rangers to recruit Barry Ferguson.

Ferguson captained both Rangers and the Scotland national team under the management of McLeish and between them the pair regularly filled the trophy cabinet at Ibrox.

One of Scotland's outstanding performers of recent years, Ferguson clocked up almost 450 games in two spells at Rangers, with a brief interlude at Blackburn Rovers in between. He is a magnificent holding midfield player capable of chipping in with vital goals.

McLeish decided it was the perfect time to present Ferguson with a new challenge at St. Andrew's and he believes his fellow Scot has the ability to add another successful chapter to his glittering career in England.

"I believe he's very capable of competing with the best players in the Premier League. For me, Barry is a midfielder at his peak," said McLeish.

"Barry has got the culture of the true-grit Brit, who will go through brick walls to play football.

"He has a winning mentality and that is proven by all the winner's medals he has won."

Factfile

Name: Barry Ferguson
Born: Hamilton, 02/02/78
Position: Midfielder
Previous clubs: Rangers, Blackburn Rovers, Rangers.

Baby Blues

The Blues' promotion back to the Premier League means boss Alex McLeish needed to look for proven quality to add to his squad to help his team compete at the highest level.

But McLeish is also keeping his eye on the club's emerging talent which is nurtured by the Academy run by Terry Westley.

Westley's Under-18 charges made it all the way through to the semi-finals of the FA Youth Cup in 2009 – their best run for 24 years.

Being back in the Premier League has seen the re-instatement of the Blues reserve side which will further help the development of young players.

And although some are released after not quite making the grade, a handful of the Blues' young professionals are starting to make their mark at first-team level, both at St. Andrew's and with other League clubs where they are benefiting from loan moves.

With a mix of new signings, established stars and homegrown talent, the future for the Blues should be bright with these youngsters to keep an eye on.

Jordon Mutch

The highly talented midfielder signed a two-year professional deal after two years as an Academy player at St. Andrew's.

A foot injury held back the England Under-17 international during the 2008/09 season but he still got a taste of first-team football in a Carling Cup tie at Southampton.

Aged just 16 years and 268 days he became the second-youngest Blues debutant after club legend Trevor Francis.

Described by Academy boss Westley as one of the top young midfielders in the country, Mutch is hoping for big things in 2010.

"This is a step further in my career. I am looking to progress on and my target is to get in the first team next year," he said.

Robin Shroot

The young winger didn't come through Birmingham's youth set-up but was snapped up by McLeish from non-league side Harrow Borough.

Shroot was given a debut in the FA Cup against Wolves before a loan spell at Walsall towards the end of the 2008/09 season and McLeish is keen for the Northern Ireland Under-21 international to follow that route again to garner further experience.

"He's unproven in League football but he's a good footballer," said the Blues boss.

"He needs to improve his speed and strength and that's why a season out on loan would be great and it would be good for us to see how he develops."

Shroot joined League Two side Burton Albion on loan for the 2009/10 season.

Jacob Rowe

The teenage defender was named as the Academy player of the year for 2008/09 and awarded a one-year professional contract at St. Andrew's.

"If anyone deserved one on sheer determination to improve it's him," said Academy coach Steve Spooner.

"He knew what he was short of and tried to do something about it by working on his weaknesses.

"The aim now is to get rid of those weaknesses that would prevent him getting near the first-team."

Mitch Mcpike

Local lad McPike has been with the Blues since the age of 11 and has now signed a professional deal running until the summer of 2011.

"This is a target I have had for some time," said the midfielder.

"Now I will keep working hard to achieve my other aims and ambitions, which ultimately are to break into the first-team and pin down a place."

Ashley Sammons

Another locally born prospect, the Solihull-based midfielder was rewarded for his progress through the Academy with a two-and-a-half-year professional deal during the 2008/09 season.

An England Under-18 international, Sammons got a taste of first-team football before that during pre-season and has sights set on more regular involvement.

"If he continues to show the desire that he has been doing he can go a long way in the game," said McLeish.

Krystian Pearce

The powerful central defender spent the 2008/09 season on loan at Scunthorpe, helping the League One side reach the play-offs and the final of the Johnstone's Paint Trophy.

Pearce got almost 50 games under his belt and was expected to go out on loan again during the 2009/10 campaign to gain further first-team experience.

Super Strikers

Master marksman Kevin Phillips led the way as West Bromwich Albion's loss proved Birmingham's gain.

Blues boss Alex McLeish snapped up the veteran frontman from the Baggies before the start of the 2008/09 season.

And while Phillips admits he would have liked to have started more games in the promotion campaign, he always came up with the goods.

Of his 14 Championship goals, only one came in a defeat and ten contributed to victories – including one in the 500th game of his career.

"He is a born finisher," enthused McLeish. "I got a quality finisher and a guy that I would have liked to have worked with a few years ago."

While 'Super Kev' is moving towards the latter stage of his 250-goal career, Cameron Jerome is still an emerging talent and McLeish believes the striker has what it takes to make his mark in the Premier League. "With his pace and power he is a handful for people," said the Blues boss.

"If Cameron can use it in the right way and make the right runs and study people like Anelka and Defoe then he's got a great future."

Factfile

Name: Kevin Phillips
Born: Hitchin, 25/07/73
Position: Striker
Championship appearances 2008/09: 24 (12 sub)
Goals: 14

Factfile

Name: Marcus Bent
Born: Hammersmith, London, 19/05/78
Position: Striker
Championship appearances 2008/09: 16 (17 sub)
Goals: 3

Factfile

Name: Cameron Jerome
Born: Huddersfield, 14/10/86
Position: Striker
Championship appearances 2008/09: 25 (18 sub)
Goals: 9

As well as Phillips and Jerome, McLeish could also call on Garry O'Connor, Marcus Bent and James McFadden to help Blues bounce back to the Premier League.

O'Connor's 2008/09 season was disrupted by injury but the Scot boasted an impressive strike-rate and scored all his goals in a winning cause.

Bent worked tirelessly when asked to lead the line and each time he found the back of the net the Blues won.

McFadden's versatility as an attacker always makes him an ace up McLeish's sleeve and when you need a goal out of the blue, the young Scot is nearly always your man.

McLeish strengthened his armoury further for the assault on the Premier League but when it came to the class of 2008/09, he was spoiled for choice.

He added: "They've all got so much quality and they all made an important contribution."

Factfile

Name: Garry O'Connor
Born: Edinburgh, 07/05/83
Position: Striker
Championship appearances 2008/09: 10 (6 sub)
Goals: 6

James McFadden

Super Mac Flying High

Flying Scotsman James McFadden is eager to grace the top-flight again after helping Blues to promotion.

McFadden has previously worked his magic in the Premier League for both Birmingham and Everton.

Relegation with the Blues in 2008 was a major blow to the Scotland international but boss Alex McLeish persuaded him to stay at St. Andrew's and fight his way back. The versatile frontman responded by playing a key part in Blues' success.

McFadden weighed in with goals at a crucial time – including a corker in the home win over Charlton – and Blues should now reap the benefits when he gets to showcase his talent again on the big stage.

"Promotion was the aim. We had plenty of belief and we achieved our goal," said McFadden. "And now we can look forward to being back in the Premier League."

Factfile

Name: James McFadden
Born: Glasgow, 14/04/83
Position: Midfielder
Championship appearances 2008/09: 22 (8 sub)
Goals: 4

Seb Larsson

At the start of the 2008/09 season, Seb Larsson's future at St. Andrew's was so uncertain that he admitted it was starting to take its toll on his performances.

But that all changed when the summer transfer window closed and the super Swede was able to devote all his energies to the Blues promotion bid.

"It was nice just to concentrate on playing football again because that's what I wanted to do," he said.

"There was some turning point where all the focus turned back on the football and obviously my performances became a bit better as well."

Larsson's commitment to the Blues cause was then never in doubt as he remained a regular selection for boss Alex McLeish.

And the former Arsenal youngster proved he would play wherever necessary to help the team by swapping his favoured right wing role for spells in centre of midfield and even at right-back.

Back in the top flight, Larsson may again get a licence to thrill and return to his attacking instincts.

No doubt plenty of goalkeepers will remember his repertoire of stunning goals from the Blues' last Premier League campaign and Larsson is confident McLeish's men will be ready to meet the challenge.

"Hopefully we can be better after a season in the Championship," added the Sweden international.

Factfile

Name: Seb Larsson
Born: Eskilstuna, Sweden, 06/06/85
Position: Midfielder
Championship appearances 2008/09: 35 (3 sub)
Goals: 1

Thanks for the Memories

Promotion to the Premier League meant changes at St. Andrew's as manager Alex McLeish looked to strengthen his squad for the battles ahead.

Inevitably that meant a few departures as well, as space was made for new signings. And no-one was wished a fonder farewell than defender Radhi Jaidi, whose three-year spell with the Blues came to an end.

The giant Tunisian was a popular figure who always gave his all as a commanding central defender as he clocked up close to 100 appearances for the Blues.

During that time the former Bolton man helped Birmingham to two promotion successes and fittingly bowed out on a high in the win over Reading which clinched a return to the top flight in the final game of the 2008/09 season.

"Radhi is a cracking guy, who has been an excellent servant to Birmingham City," said McLeish.

"He's a hard-working and dedicated professional and we all wish him well for the future."

Jaidi's international team-mate Mehdi Nafti also ended a four-year spell with the Blues, while loan men Scott Sinclair, Carlos Costly and Kemy Agustien returned to their parent clubs after playing a part in Blues' promotion success.

Defender Stephen Kelly clinched a move to Premier League rivals Fulham after falling out of favour during the promotion season at St. Andrew's.

The Irish full-back had been an ever-present for Blues in the 2007/08 campaign but moved on loan to Stoke last season before reaching the end of his contract.

Kelly agreed a three-year deal at Craven Cottage after ending a similar spell with Blues.

Factfile

Name: Radhi Jaidi
Born: Tunis, 30/08/75
Position: Defender
Championship appearances 2008/09: 30
Goals: 0

GARRY O'CONNOR

Fun & Games

Can you find the 12 words hidden in the grid?

C	H	A	A	M	C	L	E	I	S	H	Q	U	C
Q	S	U	B	P	H	M	U	R	T	S	U	N	A
U	T	R	O	H	T	I	R	S	R	B	E	D	R
I	A	S	B	I	R	M	I	N	G	L	U	R	S
F	N	A	Y	L	M	M	A	R	X	U	D	S	L
O	D	M	C	L	F	U	G	I	O	N	R	L	E
P	R	E	M	I	E	R	L	E	A	G	U	E	Y
R	E	S	O	P	I	P	U	N	D	Q	E	A	S
O	W	M	U	S	O	H	P	R	A	U	R	N	V
M	S	U	C	T	A	Y	P	H	I	M	C	B	B
L	C	H	A	M	P	I	O	N	S	H	I	P	L
Y	A	N	D	R	O	H	W	K	A	R	T	O	U
A	R	E	B	I	T	A	Y	L	O	R	M	E	E
P	R	O	M	O	T	I	O	N	N	M	A	T	S

St. Andrews
Blues
Promotion
Championship
McLeish
Carsley
Phillips
Queudrue
Taylor
Carr
Murphy
Premier League

Name that player

ANSWERS ON PAGE 61

Case for the Defence

The Blues' promotion success in 2008/09 was built on solid foundations thanks to a magnificent defensive record.

Factfile
Name: Maik Taylor
Born: Hildeshein, Germany, 04/09/71
Position: Goalkeeper
Championship appearances 2008/09: 45
Goals: 0

Perhaps not surprisingly, given manager Alex McLeish's outstanding pedigree as a top-class central defender in his playing days, Birmingham's back four was second to none.

Blues boasted the best defensive record in the Championship with just 37 goals conceded in 46 games, with only 17 of those going in at St. Andrew's. Only Sheffield Wednesday conceded fewer goals at home during the course of the season.

Goalkeeper Maik Taylor set the standard as a model of consistency as he missed just one league game thanks to a controversial sending-off against Plymouth during the promotion run-in.

The veteran Northern Ireland international gets better with age and kept 17 clean sheets as he lined up another tilt at the Premier League.

In front of him, Blues had to chop and change their defensive line-up due to injuries which made their achievement even more impressive.

Factfile
Name: Liam Ridgewell
Born: Bexley, 21/07/84
Position: Defender
Championship appearances 2008/09: 35
Goals: 1

Leading the way for appearances was Liam Ridgewell, who started 36 times in the Championship before breaking a leg in the closing stages of the season.

Factfile
Name: David Murphy
Born: Hartlepool, 01/03/84
Position: Defender
Championship appearances 2008/09: 28 (2)
Goals: 0

The central defender would miss the start of the Blues' Premier League return but McLeish was looking forward to having the former Aston Villa man back.

"This is a small crisis in his career but he will be back as strong as ever," said McLeish.

Radhi Jaidi gave his usual solid service in his final season at St. Andrew's, while Martin Taylor was back to his best as another central defensive option.

Factfile
Name: Stuart Parnaby
Born: Durham, 19/07/82
Position: Defender
Championship appearances 2008/09: 19 (2)
Goals: 0

David Murphy was a regular at left-back until a broken knee-cap curtailed his season a couple of games early, while Stephen Carr filled the problem right-back slot following Stuart Parnaby's injury and Stephen Kelly's move to Stoke.

Factfile
Name: Franck Queudrue
Born: Paris, 27/08/78
Position: Defender
Championship appearances 2008/09: 23 (2)
Goals: 3

But the surprise package was Franck Queudrue, who went from being placed on the transfer list before the season started to the club's Player of the Year.

The experienced Frenchman confounded his critics to play his way back into McLeish's plans with his versatility in the back four proving crucial to the Blues' promotion success.

Factfile
Name: Martin Taylor
Born: Ashington, 09/11/79
Position: Defender
Championship appearances 2008/09: 23 (1)
Goals: 1

Magic Johnson and Dann is the Man

The Blues' defence did a magnificent job in helping secure promotion in 2009 but boss Alex McLeish still wasted no time in strengthening his back line ready for the step up to the Premier League.

An outstanding centre-half in his playing days in Scotland, McLeish knows the art of defending inside out.

And so he had no qualms in paying a club record fee, for a defender, of £5 million to Cardiff City to secure the services of Roger Johnson.

Also moving into St. Andrew's was Coventry City's Scott Dann as McLeish dipped back into the Championship to acquire two young talents he believes have what it takes to prosper in the top flight.

Johnson, a powerful presence in both penalty areas, was widely regarded as one of the best defenders outside the Premier League as Cardiff just lost out in the race for the play-offs last season.

The former Wycombe Wanderers man played in every game bar one but his disappointment at falling short of promotion was wiped out by his move to Blues.

Factfile

Name: Roger Johnson
Born: Ashford, 28/04/83
Position: Defender
Previous clubs: Wycombe Wanderers, Cardiff City

"Premier League football is the dream at the start of any footballer's career so I am pleased I've been given the chance by Birmingham," said Johnson, who played almost 150 games in his three years in Wales.

"The aim is to stay in the Premier League and hopefully I will have a big part to play in that.

"At both clubs I have been at I have got on well with the fans and hopefully that will continue here."

Johnson's arrival ended Dann's short reign as Blues' most expensive defender as the undisclosed fee paid to Coventry was eclipsed within a fortnight during the build-up to Birmingham's Premier League return.

But that did not diminish the high regard Dann is held in by McLeish.

"Scott is another young player who wants to be the best," said the Blues boss.

Dann started his career with Walsall and started over 50 league games for the Saddlers after coming through the club's youth system.

That progress attracted the interest of Coventry, where the England under-21 international flourished further in an 18-month stint at the Ricoh Arena.

His appointment as captain last season hinted at maturity beyond his years and following another move across the Midlands, the young central defender now has the opportunity to take his game to a new level with the Blues.

Factfile

Name: Scott Dann
Born: Liverpool, 14/02/87
Position: Defender
Previous clubs: Walsall, Coventry

DAMIEN JOHNSON

QUIZ ANSWERS, FUN & GAMES SOLUTIONS

Big Blues Quiz

1 83

2 Cameron Jerome

3 Newcastle United

4 Gil Merrick

5 Honduras

6 West Ham United

7 French

8 Won his 50th cap

9 Arsenal

10 Plymouth

Wordsearch

C	H	A	A	**M**	**C**	**L**	**E**	**I**	**S**	**H**	**Q**	U	**C**
Q	**S**	U	B	**P**	H	M	U	R	T	S	**U**	N	**A**
U	**T**	R	O	**H**	T	I	R	S	R	B	**E**	D	**R**
I	**A**	S	B	**I**	R	M	I	N	G	L	**U**	R	**S**
F	**N**	A	Y	**L**	M	**M**	A	R	X	U	**D**	S	**L**
O	**D**	M	C	**L**	F	**U**	G	I	O	N	**R**	L	**E**
P	**R**	**E**	**M**	**I**	**E**	**R**	**L**	**E**	**A**	**G**	**U**	**E**	**Y**
R	**E**	S	O	**P**	I	**P**	U	N	D	Q	**E**	A	S
O	**W**	M	U	**S**	O	**H**	P	R	A	U	R	N	V
M	**S**	U	C	T	A	**Y**	P	H	I	M	C	B	**B**
L	**C**	**H**	**A**	**M**	**P**	**I**	**O**	**N**	**S**	**H**	**I**	**P**	**L**
Y	**A**	N	D	R	O	H	W	K	A	R	T	O	**U**
A	**R**	E	B	I	**T**	**A**	**Y**	**L**	**O**	**R**	M	E	**E**
P	**R**	**O**	**M**	**O**	**T**	**I**	**O**	**N**	N	M	A	T	**S**

Name that player

GARRY O'CONNOR

CAMERON JEROME

STUART PARNABY

LIAM RIDGEWELL

Spot the ball